A Graced Perspective

30 Days of Devotion

Michelle Farmer

A Graced Perspective
Copyright © 2023 by Michelle Farmer

ISBN 9798393225841

To my husband, Darren A. Farmer Sr.
&
To my children, Darren Jr. and Daylin

Thank you for loving me, inspiring me and
showing me grace. I love you all.

FOREWORD

Blessings to you my Father's children. Even in this moment, we stand grateful for the cacophony of life experiences that have birthed this baby called a "Graced Perspective." Michelle, I write this to you. You have taken life's jabs and the glitter of experience and allowed it to beautify your perspective on life and your commitment to God. Grace is one hardest things to comprehend! While it isn't necessarily the forgiveness of God, and many times referred to as the favor of God, grace is one of those things that is best shown, defined, and even experienced simply, when you don't deserve it. It's two fold! On one hand it's what you don't deserve and on the other hand it's the ability to operate in something much bigger than yourself, to bring about transformation to the place where grace is being experienced! In other words, IT'S BIGGER THAN YOU! The vision, the ministry, the book, the business, the idea is bigger than you! To the millions that will read this book, YOU ARE GRACED FOR IT! Michelle, you are graced for it! I speak, that this book will reach millions across the world and it will serve as a reminder that what God has placed inside of you is more than enough to bring change to the world. What a wonderful mother you are both spiritually and naturally. You've mastered a level of class that is unmatched in today's time. Since the age of 15, you've stood behind me, you've stood beside to support all of my endeavors! You supported them almost as if they were yours. I'm grateful that the time has come that I am now able to support you! I stand behind you, I validate you, and I am pushing you! I am believing in you! You don't have to worry, your husband will stand behind you to uplift you and to encourage your constant movement towards being the best you, you could ever be! Lastly, to everyone that will read this book, apply it to your entire life! These words weren't created from smooth plains, however they were birthed through seasons of pain that ultimately produced purpose. Take the words that are written in this book as encouragement, healthy correction, and most importantly take the words written in this book as words that will open you up to the realm of a graced perspective!

Best,
Your Husband, Apostle Darren Farmer, Sr.

DESIRE

Pray without ceasing.
1 Thessalonians. 5:17

Before embarking on any life changing journey, there must first be something that drives and pushes you to make it to the end before you even start. That something is desire. Before you continue, before you flip another page be sure that the desire to draw closer to God is there. Not for anything that He can offer or give you, but the desire to know that God hears you.

As you continue on, it is important to note that this is not another book about getting God to act as a genie in a bottle, but rather about you taking responsibility and committing yourself to praying. The overall focus is a better you. It is about you changing. It is about you growing. It is about you being more mindful. It is about you imploring God to help you become a better you.

The desire to pray cannot be fueled by the want for stuff and external changes. The desire to pray can only be fueled by wanting to understand and know God. This is what prayer is all about.

As your desire increases, the ability to pray without ceasing will become an involuntary response. You won't always have to stop to find the nearest closet or the closest church. You will be able to pray as you are walking. You will be able to pray as you are driving. You will be able to pray without ceasing.

FAITH

But without faith it is impossible to please him:
Hebrews 11:6

Let's talk about Faith. There is one verse that comes to mind when faith seems hard to maintain and that is Hebrews 11:6.

I have heard this, read it and even reiterated it to others, however, the simplicity of the words convicted me and blew my mind. Impossible, according to Merriam-Webster, means incapable of being or of occurring[1]. Let me put it plainly for you; without faith you are incapable of being pleasing to God. Yikes! That hurts, doesn't it? Trust me, it got me too in that moment. You and I were created for His good pleasure. Us being pleasing to God brings Him glory.

Faith is strictly spiritual. Why? Because faith always goes against what you see. Faith always combats what you hear. Faith always gives you strength to believe when everything in life is contrary to that which God has promised you. Faith gives you access to promises that are reserved for those who believe.

---

[1] *Definition of IMPOSSIBLE*. (2022). Www.merriam-Webster.com. https://www.merriam-webster.com/dictionary/impossible

How do I know this? Because it says so in the latter end of the verse. When the doctors are speaking sickness, faith reminds you that he is a healer. When you have sacrificed your last, faith lets you know that He is a provider. When your days get a little dark, faith lets you know that He is the light. When death is all around you, faith lets you know that He is your life . Above all else, no matter where you find yourself in life, faith lets you know who He is.

I just want to highlight the definition of impossible one more time- incapable of being.

Incapable of being what? Everything that God has called for you to be.

Without faith, you will not take the next step because it isn't clear. Without faith, you will forfeit God's will because you would rather stay comfortable. Without faith, you won't pray and trust God. Without faith, you won't trust that God actually knows best.

When we live our lives without faith, we are not living to our fullest potential. Don't put limits where God says there are none. I am encouraging you beyond what you see, feel and hear- keep the faith.

Pray with me:
Dear God, I thank you for this moment. Today I am asking that you would help my faith. Increase it and help me to constantly live with it. Every season is not easy and every step is not clear, but God I want to be pleasing to you and without faith I am incapable of doing so. I am praying for an increase in faith and the strength to walk in it.
It is so, in Jesus' name.

FORGIVE

Then said Jesus, Father, forgive them:
Luke 22:34

Jesus pardoned the actions of his accusers with these simple words. It isn't until you endure a season of crucifixion that this notion will be understood. The groundbreaking part of this whole thing is that he wasn't forgiving strangers. He was forgiving those He prayed with, those He had compassion on when others didn't. They were the same ones who spoke so highly of Him. He was the greatest.

The most powerful aspect of this level of forgiveness is forgiving those who will turn on you because they don't understand the plan of God for your life. They have to be forgiven because essentially they expedite the process of you reaching your God given potential. They have to be forgiven for your sake. Unfortunately, in the word's of Christ, "they know not what they do." They didn't believe that Jesus would rise again. They didn't believe that He would return again and have a greater love and compassion for them. They same goes for you. They don't know and that's okay. Just like they didn't understand with Jesus, they don't understand that the word over your life can not be broken because it is forever settled. So forgive them, they really didn't know that they were pushing you right into the arms of The God who understands all too well. The beauty in forgiving those who falsely accuse and mock you is they ,in the end, will acknowledge who you are, just as they did Jesus.

Pray with me:

Dear God, I thank you for this moment. I thank you for every painful situation and I even thank you for those who have hurt me. I am grateful that every negative experience has led me right to you. I pray that you would give me the strength and ability to release every individual in forgiveness. Let my heart be softened toward them. Help me to forgive just like you. It is so, in Jesus' name.

FOCUS
...think on these things.
Philippians 4:8

It can be so easy to lose focus in a never-slowing world. In a world that is insatiable. A world that is only proud of you if you are living up to their standards. When I say world, I am referring to society as a whole as well as your smaller world- your network of connections, friends, family, constituents and whoever else that may include. We feel the pressure from everywhere to try to stay focused, all while juggling everything but the kitchen sink. The only time it is ever acceptable to have everything and the kitchen sink is if we're talking cookies, however in real life it looks like confusion and chaos and that is definitely not sweet.

Focus on what is important and what is edifying to you as a whole. Research shows that we have a tendency to process, receive and dwell on negative stimuli more readily[2]. In short, we feel the sting of a rebuke more powerfully than we feel the joy of praise. Amazing, right? This is also a

---

[2] Moore, C. (2019, December 30). What Is The Negativity Bias and How Can it be Overcome? PositivePsychology.com. https://positivepsychology.com/3-steps-negativity-bias/

good reason why we so easily lose focus on what we are doing and accomplishing.

We can however, "retrain" our minds, by thinking on "these" things that Paul gives us in Corinthians. The other issue with focus is that we have two directions to focus in- on the glass being half empty or it being half full.

I cannot tell you what to do, but I would highly suggest that you think on the glass being half full. There is always something positive to think of; there's always a silver lining. It's not until you shift your focus that your views, patterns and ways of thinking will change.

Pray with me:

Dear God, thank you for this moment. I pray that you would help me to realign my focus, that I may readily acknowledge all that you are doing in my life. Help me to think on what is true in your eyes. I thank you for allowing me this moment to focus on you. Thank you for allowing my ability to focus on the positive to become me. It is so, in Jesus' name.

REMEMBER

And they remembered his words.
Luke 24:8

Have you ever found yourself in a down place and it took nothing but a reminder to get you out of that place and light a fire back within you to continue on? Same here. The mind can be a beautiful and terrible thing all at once. It is amazing that with just one reminder your entire being can be shifted and even propelled back to a reality that is greater than what you could ever imagine.

I can only imagine the whirlpool of emotions that flooded the Mary's when they were reminded of Jesus' words. To think that they found themselves in such a place of doubt and discouragement when they saw the empty tomb. The empty tomb in this moment represented an uncertain and elusive place. Just like we have those times where life is just not making sense. You don't know where you're going, you're not even sure if you're going and at this point its just time to give up and figure something else out. All of a sudden, a reminder happened. You could find it within yourself, it could come from a conversation with a stranger, it could come from the voice of your

GPS saying to you "continue on this road, you're destination is just up ahead."

It is in this moment that you remember the "why" and purpose for that desolate moment. Every hard to handle moment becomes worth it again. Your thinking becomes that much clearer. You are inspired again, this time determined to grow through the uncertainty and not let it overtake you. You remembered the word that God spoke over your life before you were formed and brought to this earth. Every word is settled. Every plan is good. Remembering His words brings you back to yourself allowing you to draw back to God and overcome every negative word, thought and situation with grace, strength and joy. Remember His words because your destiny is just up ahead.

Pray with me:

Dear God, I thank you for this moment. I thank you for every moment of weariness that has caused me to turn back to you. I ask that as I continue that you would allow for your words to ring heavy in my heart and stay at the forefront of my thoughts. Let them not be a passive and distant memory, but a core memory that will live in me forever. Allow me to feel your joy and peace every time I experience the presence of your words. It is so, in Jesus' name.

BREAKTHROUGH

...Who for the joy that was set before him endured the cross,
Hebrews 12:2

When my daughter was 9 months, we experienced the breaking through of her first tooth: which was exciting and dreadful all at the same time. It was a lot easier for my husband and I to endure with her because we knew what was coming was going to be great. We knew it meant growth, proper development and a new level in life. For her though, it meant pain, sleepless nights and plenty of crying. She was distressed because of what she was experiencing, not understanding that all that she was going through was necessary for her teeth to breakthrough.

The hardest part of breakthrough is the moment just before breakthrough happens. The fire seems the hottest. The night seems to last the longest. The weight of your assignment seems too heavy to carry. The road that you are on is the darkest it has ever been. He's pruning, refining, readjusting and preparing you for what is to come. The fire is to refine you. The pain is to remind you that He is your strength. The way got a little darker so you could run to find your light in God. All of this is just to prove God's work in you. God has so much in store for you.

God knows there is more at the end. I can assure you he is not withholding anything good from you. He is simply testing and growing your faith. At the end of it all is joy, peace, maturity, grace, love and every promise that God has to fulfill in you. He wants you to know and trust that He is right there with you. He's been exactly where you are.

Resisting is not the better choice. Giving up is not the better choice. The world needs what God is bringing out of you. Just as Jesus Broke through for you on the cross, you have to break through for yourself and those God has attached to your life. You have to breakthrough for the victory that is waiting on the other side.

Once my daughter's tooth broke through, she was at peace. She was back to smiling and laughing. The tears, the fever and the sleepless nights, were but for a moment and were absolutely worth it. The same way I encouraged her is the same way I will encourage you, " I know it hurts, but I promise, breakthrough is almost here."

Pray with me:
Dear God, I thank you for this moment. I ask now that you would continue to give me the ability to endure. I pray endurance for every test, every storm, every misunderstanding. That I may come out strengthened and better. I know that every thing will work for my good, because that is how you planned it.
It is so, in Jesus' name.

WORDS

Death and life are in the power of the tongue:
Proverbs 18:21

Every word that you speak holds weight.
From the prepositions to the nouns to the
verbs, every single word matters.
I had the pleasure of being able to nurse
both of my children for their first year of
life. Around month 10 with my daughter, I
started saying things like:
"I don't think I want to do this anymore."
"I don't think my body can take this."
"I think its time for her to just use the
bottle."
"She's eating regular food, so she doesn't
need me."
Slowly, but surely, my body started to
respond to what was being said out of my
mouth. The extra bags of milk were no
more. Nursing 4-5 times a day was no more.
Supplying for my daughter was no more.
Then that small voice whispered to me,
" YOU spoke this dry place."
 I could have cried when I heard this,
simply because it was the truth. This season
of my life came because of my words. That
voice whispered just one more time:
"Imagine the overflow you could've had, if
only you had spoken it."

I could've cried AGAIN! I could only imagine how many times I unintentionally spoke myself out of receiving the abundance that God had for me. I gathered myself quickly and assured myself and God, that would be the last time I ever self-sabotaged.

Your words matter. From the biggest to the smallest- pay attention to what you are really saying. Oftentimes, we blame our circumstances on the adversary or someone else, when in all actuality, we did it ourselves. We spoke out of our mouths and everything around us responded. Not only that, but our body and spirit responded. Rather than saying to the mountain be thou removed, we spoke that the mountain would be too great for us and would eventually crush us, so that's what it did.

You find yourself lost because you have spoken that you are confused and don't understand . You find yourself running from his love because you have spoken that God couldn't love you. You find yourself missing out on the overflow because you speak yourself into dry places.

Before you speak another word, think of all that you have missed out on because of your words. Let your words be what invites God's blessings into your life and not what pushes them away. Your life depends on the words that you speak. Let your words line up with His word and watch Him have His perfect work in your life.

Pray with me:

Dear God, thank you for this moment. I pray that you would help me to be mindful of my words. Help me to speak what is good and according to your word. I pray that when I cannot find the words to say that I would find solace and truth in yours.

It is so, in Jesus' name.

REFLECTIONS

*As in water face answereth to face, so the heart of
man to man.*
Proverbs 27:19

Reflections can be such a beautiful thing. It allows us to see ourselves from our own perspective. When you take time to reflect and analyze you give yourself the opportunity to fix those things that aren't right. At a surface level, you are checking for anything that's not presentable; that one piece of hair that needs an extra brush through, the dry lips you earn after brushing your teeth, the stain on your shirt that you didn't notice and is now screaming at you and the list goes on.

You make note of all those things and take the necessary steps to correct them; you grab that brush, put on that chapstick and as much as you don't feel like it, you change that shirt. You have made yourself presentable and acceptable in your eyes first, so when you meet the eyes of others, they will see the same. There is nothing you need to worry about because you took time out of your day to look at your reflection and correct what may have been out of place or not up to standard.

We often forget one major check when viewing our reflection and that is our heart. We look great on the outside, but there is always something on the inside that needs tending to. This check however, cannot be done on our own. We need God to reveal to us who we truly are; He is the only one that knows, after all. It is our heart that reveals who we really love, not just with words, but in deed and truth. It reveals what is most important to us. Whatever your heart is filled with is what will come out of you.

Everyday as you are starting, going throughout and ending your day, ask God to show you your heart, He will show you. When He shows you those things that do not reflect Him, get guidance on how to change and stay committed until what you are practicing becomes you.

Ask God to show you your reason for posting on social media. Ask Him to show you why you talk down on yourself. Ask Him to show you why it is hard for you to rejoice with others. Seek Him to find your true self. He is the only one that can search our hearts, know it, and replace it with one that can be full of Him. When your heart's perspective is changed you can help change someone else's.

When you make time for this necessary check, you will have nothing to worry about because when man sees you they will see someone who's heart is filled with the spirit of God. You will reflect joy. You will reflect peace. You will reflect hope. You will reflect the Grace of God that is free to all who will receive it. You will reflect your father who is in heaven. What a beautiful reflection you will be.

Pray with me:
Dear God, I thank you for this moment. I thank you for this time to reflect and speak to you. I ask that you would search my heart and help me to face anything in it that is unlike you. Help me to see myself the way you see me. Help people to see your characteristics when they see me. Thank you for softening and changing my heart day by day.
It is so, in Jesus' name.

WISDOM

If any of you lack wisdom, let him ask of God,
James 1:5

I know that I am not the only one who has heard that "wisdom comes with age", which can be true, however, your age does not determine how wise you actually are. In all reality, the amount of wisdom you possess is based upon whether you have asked of God to give it to you. Wisdom is given to all those who ask.

Isn't that amazing? All you have to do ask. Here is why wisdom is necessary for those of all ages- you need it to grow. You need it to make sound life decisions. You need it to follow the voice of God. It is more than understanding; wisdom allows you to properly apply all that you know. Don't be afraid to ask. God is waiting to bestow you with His wisdom.

When you ask and God gives, do not let anyone decry what has been granted to you. At the age of 27, I already had 3 of those silver strands of wisdom. My initial reaction was to dye them IMMEDIATELY, but then I remembered I asked for this wisdom and earned every bit of it. I also quickly embraced them when I realized they are a beautiful crown of glory (proverbs 16:31).

He knows all, not you or I! The same way I ask for wisdom and I receive it, is the same way it can happen for you.

God can send His wisdom in many different forms. It can come from a person who has been where you are. It can come from an experience. It can come from a test in life. It can come straight from His word. However God sends it, receive it. Let this be the last day that you operate without God's wisdom because you were under the impression that it was not readily accessible to you. Ask your father for it and receive it.

Pray with me:
Dear God, I thank you for this moment. I thank you for the ability to ask anything in your name. Today I ask that you would give me wisdom. Let the wisdom that you give me be used to make me better. I pray that you would give me the maturity that I need to handle the wisdom that you are bringing to me.
It is so, in Jesus' name.

WITNESS

A true witness delivereth souls:
Proverbs 14:25

A few years ago, I was in a very low state. I was hurt. I was tired. I believed that I wasn't enough for God and that God wanted nothing to do with me. I reached the point where I told God not to bother with me because He was wasting his time. I reached this place by believing more of what people thought of me than what God thought of me. I was that person in church who literally just came to sit and look.

My husband and I were driving around DC when I heard very clearly, "Michelle, don't leave me. Give me another chance. I won't let you die here." Imagine that, the God who controls all, asking me, a nobody, to give Him another chance. I told my husband that I was going to Church that Sunday and you will not believe what happened. I got there as the pastor was getting up to preach (I was pretty down y'all, so I told myself I was only going for the word, sorry praise team.) and midway through his sermon he says "You can't die here, your promise is coming."

I cried the ugliest cry in that moment because I came to the realization I had truly experienced God and His grace.

In other words, I am encouraging you the same way God encouraged me. I am encouraging you to come out of the low state. There are people who need what you have. You are more than enough because you are chosen by God. You are because He IS.

Your version of grace will not be my version. God's covering of grace is individualized, tailor-made to fit the story He has written for you. You may have done a lot of wrong or even tried to convince God that you were not worth His time, but God can use that for His glory. I was made a witness and God wants to make you His witness too. Don't stay away from Him. Don't stay bound. Don't stay lost. Grace is here for you.

Pray with me:
Dear God, I thank you for this moment. I thank you for your grace that is free to all. I pray that you would help me to experience a new grace for this space of my life. I thank you for the opportunity to be a witness to someone else of the power of your grace.
It is so, in Jesus' name.

REST

...For so he giveth his beloved sleep.
Psalm 127:2

Rest is necessary. Not just for our physical well being, but for our mental and spiritual health. My periods of rest give me a chance to refocus, receive further direction and have much needed prayer and meditation. This is my time to listen to what God has to say concerning where I am and where I am going. I want everything I do to be God orchestrated. I have learned the hard way that when I operate without Him, it is truly in vain.

God lead me to read psalms 127 and I have never been the same. I do not speak without God. I do not move without God. I was not created to live a life in vain, but I was created to live a life that is pleasing to Him. I was created for His good pleasure and not my own. I still have my moments, like anybody else, but in those moments I resort to rest. I have learned and understand that while I rest, He works.

One of my favorite definitions of rest according to Webster is "to sit or lie fixed or supported." When I take a moment to sit and rest, God steps in and supports me with His grace that is most sufficient. It is there in my sitting and resting that God reminds me that His yoke is easy and His burden is light and that I can always come to Him for rest when the way gets to heavy or burdensome. It is there in my sitting and resting that God reminds me of His goodness towards those that take time to seek Him (Lamentation 3:25).

Life has a way of throwing so much at you at one time that you become overtaken by the spirit of weariness. We have seen that if you're not constantly doing, you are being unproductive, but I would beg to differ. Rest is productive. One thing I have stood confidently in, if God is not doing it, I am not forcing it.

Take the necessary rest so God can, first, work on you and then work through you. When He does it, it cannot fail. When He does it, it will not be in vain but for His glory.

Pray with me:

Dear God, I thank you for this moment. I thank you for your promise of rest. I ask that you would help me to take full advantage of what resting in you has to offer. I pray that while I rest you would continue to work on my behalf. It is so, in Jesus' name.

LIGHT

As long as I am in the world, I am the light of the world.
John 9:5

If you read that and it didn't spark something within you, hold tight and keep reading. I will try my best to light that fire.

Jesus is declaring himself to be the light that John was referring to in John 1. The light that shines in darkness that can not be comprehended. The same light that was also life for every man. He is that light. However, He is the light of the world, as long as He is in the world. So how is He maintaining His light without being here physically on earth?

He does it through you and me! We are now the light because His spirit lives within us. We are the candles being put on display for all to see. We are the light of His glory meant to shine before men. We are that city on a hill, so bright and full of life.

As long as YOU are in the world, there will be light. As long as you stay connected to the source of all your power you will stay lit. Your light shines when you are doing your part and fulfilling the word of God for your life. Your light shines when you are obedient. Your light shines when you extend forgiveness to the one who you think is least deserving in your life. Your light shines when darkness is all around and you choose to stand on the fact that greater is He that is in you than he that is in the world.

You cannot be a light and be afraid. You can no longer know that you are a light and stay turned off. Flip that switch up and get to work. The world needs to see you shining! Say this with me, as long as I am in the world, I am a light for the world. God has graced you with His light and it is time for you to let it shine.

It can be so easy to dim our light to succumb to darkness. No matter how hard it gets, keep shining.

Pray with me:
Dear God, I thank you for this moment. I thank you for the opportunity to shine for you. I ask that you would help me to shine in the darkest of places that all would be drawn to you. I thank you for every opportunity I have to be used by you. For every opportunity that I have missed, I ask your forgiveness.
It is so, in Jesus' name.

LISTEN

And the LORD answered me, and said,
Habakkuk 2:2

You are motivated and you've got the momentum and that is wonderful. I am here to tell you to SLOW DOWN.

Yes, slow down. Even the greatest of runners stretch before attempting any race. They also pace themselves to give themselves a greater chance at winning. Everything that God gives you is not always for now and it is not always just for you.

Habakkuk needed answers, direction and encouragement, much like us, so he cried out to God. Whatever it is, whatever you are in need of... GO TO GOD. He has the perfect answer every time. Be sure to ponder the words of God in your heart. This season of your life is not about operating out of your own strength. It is about learning and heeding to God's voice. As you listen, grab a pen and a good notebook (upon tables) and write what God is saying. Every dream, vision, thought, answered prayer and question- write it down. It could be just for you or it could be for someone else. What you write can be the reason someone doesn't give up.

I would also like to encourage you to be vigilant and patient. This part is very important because everything will not be given right away, but I can assure you that whatever God speaks to you or shows you, whatever He has created you to do will come to past in His time and that's a promise.

Pray with me:
Dear God, I thank you for this moment. Help me to take the time to hear what you are saying. Help me to be patient as I am seeking your voice.
It is so, in Jesus' name.

TRAP AND TRANSFORM

And bringing into captivity every thought to the obedience of Christ;
2 Corinthians. 10:5

Let me start by saying this, you, with the leading and direction of the spirit of God, are the only one who can control who you become. It is not up to me or anyone else. Yes, God will send people in your life to assist and encourage you on your journey, but ultimately, you are the only one responsible for allowing God's will and purpose to be fulfilled in your life. You are the only one who can decide that changing your mind will change your life. You can change your mind by doing two things: Trap and transform.

Trap what? Your thoughts. Anything that goes against God's word for your life. Any pattern that you have created to keep yourself from growing. Any thoughts of unforgiveness that have caused you to operate in pride. This verse encourage us to trap any thought and imagination that tries to assert itself over God. I am gently reminding you that those thoughts are not so. You are not what "they" said. You are whole. You are healed. You are walking in a life of productivity and blessings. You are that word that God has spoken over your life. So trap anything else that goes contrary to His words for your life.

Once you trap, you can transform. Your transformation starts in your mind.

In order for you to fulfill God's will and have it displayed for everyone to see, you have to think like your father in heaven. Transform by replacing forgiveness with bitterness. Transform by replacing hate with love. Transform by replacing your righteousness for His.

Transform by focusing your attention to His promise. Transform by believing that God is who He says He is. Transform by remembering that as you do His will, He is with you.

Don't wait, because you don't know what tomorrow will hold. Trap anything that is not true and slows your growth. Let your mind be continuously transformed.

Pray with me:
Dear God, I thank you for this moment. I take the time to trap any negative thoughts and transform them with your words. As I trap anything that goes against your will, I will continue to transform into your likeness. It is so, in Jesus' name.

ALWAYS

And, lo, I am with you alway;
Matthew 28:20

Have you ever found yourself in a place where you are asking God "where am I?"
The road that you are on starts to become blurred. The way seems strange and you feel distant. I have been there before and while in that place, God led me to this verse.

I was quite unclear on how the great commission would be any help to me, so I reread and took time to meditate until it made sense. In true God fashion, He revealed and here was the answer:

When I reveal myself in a new way, DO NOT DOUBT, it is really me, just a new side for your next level. (V.17)

Do not forget I AM the power you need. (V.18)

I have given your assignment. I have set the mandate. Do now what I have called for you to do.(V.19)

Use what I have given you to bless someone else. (V.20)

I am with you alway. No matter how elusive, strange or dark- I AM THERE.

And he seals all of this with the promise of all promises- AMEN (it is so, so shall it be.)

Pray with me:
Dear God, I thank you for this moment. I thank you for this time to acknowledge all that your word is reminding me. I thank you for being with me even through my doubts. Please strengthen me with your word today.
It is so, in Jesus' name.

SUBMISSION
...But by love serve one another.
Galatians 5:13

A few weeks ago my husband kept asking me for floss. He did this everyday for about 2 weeks and each time I said no. After a while, he stopped asking because I didn't have what he needed. About a week after he stopped asking, I went to Target. In the midst of my shopping, my daughter started getting restless, so I stopped into the nearest aisle to settle her. When I looked up, I was standing right in front of the floss. There was a small voice within that whispered, "Get the floss." I grabbed more for the house and one for my purse.

A few days passed by and my husband finally popped the big question, "do you have any floss in your purse?" And with so much gladness I was able to say yes and in that moment, be the answer to what he was looking for. Now, the story does not end here. I asked God what I was supposed to get out of it and this is what he gave me: this is what submission looks like. It's seeing a need and filling it. It's thinking of others before yourself. It's taking that extra step to show you care and that you are listening. It's a level of love that is shown and not just verbalized. Me fulfilling this need for my Husband prompted him to do something for me I wasn't expecting. Submission is not hard or daunting, on the contrary it is very rewarding. Submission is a give-give! You cannot lose! Submission takes faith to know that even though you may not get things right the first or second time around, there is always another chance waiting right around the corner. It's not about perfection, it's all about adjusting and becoming a better you.

Submission also requires action. God won't move unless you take the first step. The same way we submit in the natural is the same way it works in the spirit. We give God our best and he gives us better.

Pray with me:
Dear God, thank you for this moment. I thank you for the opportunity to submit myself to your will and to your way. Help me to humbly submit that I may serve you and those around me well. It is so, in Jesus' name.

PROCESS

And it came to pass in the process of time.
Exodus 2:23

I remember the day when these words spoke to me. I remember being so on fire for God. I remember wanting to go forth to the nations because certain gifts and abilities I had in the spirit were confirmed. I remember feeling entitled to think the thought, that since God called me, I must be used to maximum capacity at this very moment. I remember the way this scripture humbled me and matured me. I remember God asking the question, "If I give you everything now, what will you have learned?" I pondered this question for a while, but I soon understood. If God is the author of time and is, in essence, time, himself, we cannot rush time. If we cannot rush time, then we also understand and surmise that we cannot rush God or speed things along just because we are excited. When God is doing something great within you, it has to be matured and proven in time through process.

Sometimes we can get so excited and feel like we are ready to handle the things God has promised us that we forget, one, you cannot rush time and ,two, you cannot avoid your process.

No one who is chosen by God was given the easy way out. There will be some hardness endured. There will be tests. There will be many hard lessons, but this is all apart of the process. Process can be defined as a series of actions or steps taken in order to achieve a particular end[3]. In shirt, every step you take is necessary to reach your expected end. It is not enough for you to know that God has a plan for you, but the process is essential for you. It is there to keep you humble. It is there to give you a heart of gratitude for the ways of God. The process is there to prove that His grace is sufficient. So, while the expected end will soon be realized, it can only be realized in time through the process.

Pray with me:
Dear God, I thank you for this moment. I thank you that your timing is perfect. I ask that you would help me to learn from every step of the process you have for me. Help me to embrace that you have given me the grace for this process and in time I will continue to see more of your plan manifest in my life.
It is so, in Jesus' name.

---

[3] "Process." Cambridge Dictionary, dictionary.cambridge.org/dictionary/english/process. Accessed 22 May 2022.

IT IS SO

Amen.
Revelation 22:21

The very last word of the Bible to sum it all up and conclude every matter within it is 'amen'.
Seems like such a small word to put behind such immense writings. However it is God literally settling His words in heaven forever. Not only that it confirms and affirms the Grace of God being with us all.
Amen is commonly used after a prayer or statement to express solemn ratification or agreements. It means "it is so" or "so it is."[4]

Amen is you putting action behind your words. It is confirming. It is releasing on earth what has already been released in heaven. It is confidence in knowing that God will do just what he promised.
 Amen is such a serious thing that it should cause you to use caution when choosing the words that you put before it. It's not about praying what you want but it is truly about praying what is best for you and what God actually wants for your life.

---

[4] "Amen Definition & Meaning." Merriam-Webster, www.merriam-webster.com/dictionary/amen. Accessed 2021.

It wasn't until I started saying it is so that I actually saw what I was saying.

So consider this your "know better, do better" moment. Don't just say amen because it is the thing to say- declare it confidently. Over your family, over your health and even over your mind. The list goes on and on.
As you pray today and everyday hereafter, believe it, declare it, walk in it and know, it is so and so it is.

Pray with me:
Dear God, I thank you for this moment. I thank you for this time to reflect and pray to you. I ask that you would help me to be careful in choosing my words. Help me to pray those things that line up with your will. Help me to have patience when waiting to receive every promise in you.
It is so, in Jesus' name..

REPENTANCE

So the LORD blessed the latter end of Job more than his beginning...Job 42:12

We have all heard the story of Job time and time again and unfortunately, our summation of the whole book is "Job got double for his trouble," which is true, but we miss one important detail- Job had to repent.

Not Job, the upright man, the one who was highly favored and blessed of God. Deep down inside of job was that sneaky little thing called self-righteousness. He had it all together, the beautiful wife, the wonderful children, the best of houses and cattle. Somewhere along the line though, Job lost sight of who allowed for all of these things to be. While he never cursed God, it now makes sense why Job had to endure all that He did because He needed to remember who God is.

In the middle of his going though, Job felt much like many of us, that he of all people, he should not be dealing with this. He goes on and on; HE fed the poor, HE kissed the babies to soothe them, HE donated to the poor, He did it all. Job really had a "you are getting beside yourself, sir" moment. So much so, God had to come and get him together and show just a glimpse of his track record. How it humbled Job. He had to remind job who He was. In true childlike fashion, job retreated and repented for his moment of weakness. Then and only then did God restore to him, double for his trouble. Technically, he did not get double for the trouble, he got double because he remembered who his provider was. That self righteousness that was hiding within Job was exposed and corrected and it was because of that, God was able to bless him with what He already had in store for him.

Sometimes its not just enough to be ready to receive with our mouths and actions, but we really have to be ready to receive with our hearts. Oftentimes, we find ourselves in a "proving" situation. It seems like everything is falling apart, we have no control over any of our circumstances and our petition to God is much like Job, attempting to prove why He shouldn't have allowed this. I can only imagine God looking at us saying- "This is why. You're self-righteousness has become greater than my righteousness. You have forgotten that you are because I AM. You have because I provide."

In that moment is your time to either stay concerned with 'I' or to humble yourself before almighty God and repent. It is the key to receiving what is on the other side. Always remember that your righteousness is as filthy rags, it will never compare to God.

Pray with me:
Dear God, I thank you for this moment. I thank you for this time of reflection. Help me to acknowledge and rectify anything that is unlike you. I know that I am because of you. I ask of your forgiveness for anytime that I have forgotten who you are in my life. Continue to make me better.
It is so, in Jesus' name.

PROGRESS

...set thine heart to understand...
Daniel 10:12

Daniel is a wonderful model of a sustainable and effective prayer life. He is also a wonderful example of how prayer advances us in ways we could never imagine.

Progress means moving forward; to develop to a higher, better or more advanced stage.[5]

How do we see this being defined in Daniel's life?

Daniel went from interpreting dreams to having dreams of his own to seeing visions to experiencing supernatural and angelic encounters as he continued in prayer. He continues to move forward and experience things in the spirit in an increasing extent and severity. Not just in the spiritual but the natural as well. Daniel became the most powerful man next to the king, he gained favor with man because of prayer.

You see, God's communication with us progresses based on the progress of our spiritual maturity. Meaning certain encounters will not be had because of a

---

[5] *"Progress Definition & Meaning."Merriam-Webster, www.merriam-webster.com/dictionary/progress. Accessed May 2023.*

lack of prayer or maturity in prayer. Daniel did not pray for personal gain and advancement from God, he prayed to understand the things of God and even the heart of God.

With each new level of understanding came an unlocking of another level of spiritual experience and favor. God continued to elevate Daniel in the natural and spiritual. He took care of Daniel, because Daniel remained mindful of the things of God and he honored that above all, prayer is what is needful.

Sometimes progress looks like focusing on one thing for an extended period of time. At one point, we see Daniel praying and it takes 21 days of seeking God before he hears anything. He did not pray and say it is in the hands of God now, no, he continued to pray until he received his response. We must do the same, I know it may seem like God doesn't care or maybe we convince ourselves that this request is too small and we can figure it out ourselves, but God wants to hear you. Keep praying until you see your progress.

Pray with me:

Dear God, I thank you for this moment. I pray that you would help me to make progress as I pray. I thank you for the ways you have opened me up to the things of the spirit. I ask that you would continue to mature and develop me as I pray.
It is so, in Jesus' name.

COMPLAINING

And when the people complained, it displeased the LORD:
Numbers 11:1

Have you ever been at a fine restaurant with someone and all is going well until you sit down. They start complaining about the water. They don't like how dark it is. The broccoli is too hard. They find a reason to keep having the waiter run back and forth. They ask for a well-done steak and get upset about it hurting their jaw. As you sit across from them, you think to yourself that this is the last time you will ever eat out with them. No one enjoys a complainer. Complaining is such a terrible habit that we have all partaken in from time to time. For some, it is something that is done all the time. There are some people in your life that are just never satisfied and can find the negative in any and everything. Maybe you are that person. If complaining is an issue for you, there is hope.

We essentially find it easier to complain when we don't think there is anything to be grateful for, but please note, there is ALWAYS something to be grateful for.

The children of Israel had it all made and they still found something to complain about. They were on their way to the promised land and somehow managed to complain about the journey. I believe that we have all entertained the idea that life isn't perfect, but deep down you really think it should be. The path should be easy. Money should just find you. That degree should guarantee the highest paying job. That spouse should offer limitless satisfaction. However, such is life, this typically is not the case. Sometimes, money is a struggle. Sometimes, your spouse just doesn't get it. Sometimes, that degree guarantees nothing. It is in the 'sometimes' that we find it appropriate or even necessary to complain. We forget all else that has been done or accomplished and without even thinking resort to woe is me.

Whatever moments you find yourself in on the way to the promise, don't complain. Keep in mind that all things are working together for your good. Whenever you feel that need to complain, stop and think about the bigger picture. If you're sitting at that steakhouse, think about enjoying the company you're with and how your complaining would ruin that. Find gratitude that God has placed you here to get you to your promise.

Pray with me:
Dear God, I thank you for this moment. I thank you for every opportunity and moment that is

leading me to my promise. Forgive me for every time that I complained against you and your will for my life. Help me to be grateful in all things.
It is so, in Jesus' name..

SINCERITY

*Sincerity, sound speech, that cannot be
condemned…*
Titus 2:7

I once heard someone say that every joke is
fifty percent serious. I am not sure of how
true this is, but what I do know is anything
wrapped with sarcasm is one hundred
percent offensive. Sarcasm is envy's best
friend. Think about every time you have
been sarcastic towards someone or
someone has been towards you, there was
something there beyond the joke. While
subtle, it is still very noticeable. It is almost
an unsaid hatred coming from within.
Sarcasm is deep. Sarcasm is like a bad
fragrance- the opening notes are soft and
not too overpowering. It's the dry-down
that reveals an overwhelmingly dark side
that will have you running to find the
nearest shower.

I was watching two people engage in
conversation and it was an extremely
uncomfortable sight. Every single remark
that they made to each other was wrapped
in sarcasm accompanied by an insincere
laughing eye roll. They call each other
friend, but something wasn't right. After a
while, I understood that both of them were

jealous of each other for their own separate reason. One has a degree the other doesn't. One has purchased a house the other hasn't. One has a newer car the other doesn't. They were projecting their dissatisfaction with their own life on to each other all in the name of sarcasm. This type of conversation is unfruitful. It only causes you to mishandle people rather than dealing with yourself. Watch yourself and whether or not you speak sincerely. God want us to have pure and sound speech.

Pray with me:
Dear God, I thank you for this moment. I ask that you would keep a sincere heart within me. Let whatever comes out of my mouth be a reflection of you. I ask your forgiveness for anytime I have shown hate with my use of words. Help me to be sincere in all that I say. It is so, in Jesus' name..

EXCUSES

Before I formed thee in the belly I knew thee...
Jeremiah 1:5

I debated heavily about including this part in here. Not because
I didn't think it was necessary, but because I know that this is something that hits hard. The biggest issue I find with excuse making, from myself, as well as other, is that every excuse that we make for ourselves is valid. For example, when writing this book, I told myself countless times that there is no way I could write a great book because I've never written one before...Valid. Another example can be taken right from the verse above, Jeremiah told God he couldn't be used because he was a kid... Valid. Moses, when told to tell Pharaoh the words of The Lord, said he couldn't because he was not an eloquent orator... Valid. While each of these excuses is valid, it is essentially a way to go against God's plan.

Excuses are simply a battle against God's truth. They are the weapons we use in our fight to accept who we are in Christ.

God loves us so much that He has a solution to any and every excuse that you could try to offer. I want to encourage you with this, the number of ways that you find yourself to be inadequate does not matter to God. He has already taken note of each of these ways and included those in His plan before you were formed. Before you even knew what an excuse was, He had the answer.

Pray with me:
Dear God, I thank you for this moment. I ask that you would help me to realize and accept who I am in you. Help me to see myself the way you see me. Help me to find strength in you and fight past every excuse that tries to keep me from fulfilling my purpose. Help me to remember you know me and the plans you have for me.
It is so, in Jesus' name.

BEAUTY

He hath made every thing beautiful in his time…
Ecclesiastes 3:11

Beauty can be defined as particularly graceful and excellent. Beauty is not something that can be manufactured. It is not something that can be bought. It is not something that can be faked. Beauty is literally who you are made to become.

My sister took a pottery class in high school and expressed it was her least favorite form of art. She explained that it took meticulous work- Kneading the clay, pounding the clay, all while trying to be gentle enough to create something beautiful. All of this was necessary to get rid of any air bubbles that could potentially destroy the pottery as it goes through the oven. If there were any air bubbles the pottery piece would break under the pressure of the heat, not only ruining itself, but potentially ruining the other pieces around it.

Everything that has happened in your life has been to shape you. Good and bad. Beautiful and ugly. Sad and happy. Everything has happened for a reason. Every season, trial, failed relationship, and late night was made to test your faith, work your patience and give you experience. Everything that you have gone through was to make you beautiful. God has literally been shaping and molding you. He is taking His time to make sure every air pocket and bubble is worked out. He is holding you in His hands-molding, shaping, contouring, squeezing and flattening you. He is taking His time to ensure that when you go through the fire, you will not break. You will not crack. You will not cause harm to those around you. You will come out understanding the reason for the bending and the beatings. It was all for your good.

Go through every fiery furnace with grace knowing that you'll be made pure gold, knowing that you will be the finest piece of pottery on the market and knowing that God is God enough to have the perfect plan in place for your life.

Pray with me;
Dear God, I thank you for this moment. I ask that you would continue to beautify me in your time. Help me to rest in you as I go through every trial and storm. Help me to go through

with grace that I may come out better than before.
It is so, in Jesus' name.

RELEASE

Loose him, and let him go.
John 11:44

I have read and heard the story of Lazarus a thousand times over and I'm sure you have to. I promise not to bore you. As I was reading the story of Lazarus this particular time, the emphasis that was placed on these six words was like nothing I had ever experienced with this story. It was such a fresh experience.

Typically, we end on the note that Lazarus was called by name and was made alive again by the word of God, but this time God gave me these words: "I will never leave you undone." In other words, it is not just enough for you to come back to life, but you have to be released from everything that would keep you from moving forward or even serve as a reminder of who you once were. What am I saying? The guilt you feel from past mistakes, must loose and let you go. The shame you feel from bad decisions, must loose and let you go. The belief in the thought that it could never be you, must loose and let you go. Anything from your past, even if it happened yesterday, that wants to keep you bound, must loose and let you go.

God knew what He was doing when He called you from the grave that day. He knew that it was not just enough to call you back, but he had to release you from anything that looked like death. He has given you the permission and right to be released and to walk in freedom.

Pray with me:
Dear God, I thank you for this moment. I thank you for the moment that you called me from the grave and gave me the permission to be free from my past. Help me to continue to walk in freedom knowing it is my divine right. It is so, in Jesus' name.

PROMISES

To sit under his vine and his fig tree (enjoying peace and prosperity in the kingdom).
Zechariah 3:10

I prayed a prayer recently that God would show me that He is still the God of the universe. One of the stipulations to that prayer was that God would allow me to find money. That may seem like a weird request, but I have good reason. I have never been the one to just find money or have a random monetary blessing come my way. I've received money for my birthday and Christmas, but nothing truly "unexpected." I have never seen money just sitting on the ground. Instead I was always the one losing money and blessing someone else. So this particular day, I said within my heart, "Lord, I want to find money that is blowing in the wind just for me." I left it there and kept on going. We were at the DC Botanical Gardens one day and I saw there was a children's garden and felt the need to check it out. Of course, we stayed longer than intended once my children saw you could plant seeds and water them. I was sitting under a fig tree and saw something blowing in the wind. As soon as someone walked past, it stopped. This happened two more times before I finally got up to see what it was. Lo and behold, it was money!

$90, to be exact, blowing in the wind just for me. I was so proud of my $90 because it was literally given to me by God. Now, the other part of this story is the fig tree. I had to look up exactly what a fruit bearing fig tree meant. It is a symbol of peace and prosperity. Sitting under a fruitful fig tree is literally the ability to rest in the promises of God. God has a way of going above and beyond when it comes to answering the prayers of His children. It wasn't enough to to just send the money, but He had to show me through the fig tree that His promises truly never cease to be.

Pray with me:
Dear God, I thank you for this moment. I thank you for this time to reflect on every promise that has come to pass in my life. I ask that you would continue to show yourself to be the God of the universe. With even the smallest reminders I will give thanks. Help me to stay encouraged knowing that every promise in you is sure.
It is so, in Jesus' name.

THINK

Be transformed by the renewing of your mind.
Romans 12:2

Thinking is a powerful tool. Thoughts are a powerful tool. The ability to control the thoughts you choose to believe is an even more powerful tool. I have learned that you can control your thinking patterns. It isn't just about ignoring the negative that you encounter, but your perception and where you choose to put your focus.

If you focus on what is negative, you find yourself prone to thinking on the negative side of your experiences. On the contrary, if you focus on the positive and those things that God says are true, you will find yourself having a more positive outlook on what you are experiencing.

You will have challenges. You will have moments where it seems like the truth of God is non-existent in your life. You will have moments that have you questioning your purpose. But the good news is, you do not have to become what is happening to you. What you can do, is learn from it. What you can do, is grow from it. What you can do, is remember that ALL things work together for the good of them who are the called. You are called, so it is all working for your good.

WAIT

But they that wait upon the LORD shall renew their strength;
Isaiah 40:31

Waiting wouldn't be so hard if it wasn't so hard. When I think of those like Joseph or david and even Jesus, I absolutely love how it all works out for them in the end, but the wait before the promise, was certainly not easy. David had to fight lions, bears AND Goliath before becoming the king. Joseph was sold off by his brothers, thrown in jail, lied on and accused of trying to take the king's wife before becoming one of the most powerful men in the land. Jesus had to endure persecution, false accusations and take on the sins of the world before He could reign as king.

Maybe you are not fighting bears or being thrown in jail or having to carry the weight of the world on your shoulders, but you do feel the pressure mounting as you wait. You knew it wouldn't be a breeze, but you never imagined that you would have to endure some of the things that you have endured.

Waiting is never easy, but God promises to renew our strength while waiting on Him to fulfill His promises in our life. We will not grow weary. We will not faint, because the wait will be worth it.

Pray with me:

Dear God, I thank you for this moment. I pray now that you would give me the strength as I wait on you. The strength to remain faithful. The strength to be at peace with what you allow. The strength to trust you. I thank you for the wait and stand firm on the belief that what is to come will be worth it.

It is so, in Jesus' name.

HUMILITY

Humble yourselves in the sight of the Lord, and he shall lift you up.
James 4:10

You never know how you will act in the new until you are there. New job. New house. New luxury car. With every promotion and elevation comes one of two choices- to respond with humility and gratefulness or to respond with a spirit of entitlement. Before you make a choice, let me remind you that God owes you nothing. When we humble ourselves before God, He does the exalting and when He does it, no man can take it away.

By our second year of marriage, my husband and I had built ourselves up pretty well. We had a 6-figure income, the cars of our dreams and the *ultra-* luxury apartment to go with it. However, we forgot to keep the one who allowed it all first. While we loved God and honored Him outwardly, we certainly believed that God's exalting meant stuff and we quickly learned that was not the case. In true God fashion, we withstood a major humbling whirlwind. Through that storm, we learned humility. Through that storm, we learned it was never about the things that you have that make you great. More importantly, we learned, whatever you do without God will not last.

As God blesses, promotes, prepares tables and does the exceeding abundantly in your life, be intentional about how you choose to respond. I will give it to you as plainly as God gave it to me: a chair is just a chair until you make it a throne.

Pray with me:
Dear God, I thank you for this moment. I ask now God that you would prepare me for what you have prepared for me. Help me not to misuse it. Help me to remember that all I have is because of you. I will be sure to bless your name as you bless me.
It is so, in Jesus' name.

PRAY

And I am come for thy words.
Daniel 10:12

When you think of a first responder, you think of someone who is immediately dispatched to come to your aid. Someone who puts their life at risk for the chance of saving yours. They come with an urgency, with their main goal to give you answers to the problems you may find yourself in and to reassure you that you will be okay.

Naturally, we summons our first responders with a phone call. Spiritually, we summons them with a different type of call. That call is prayer. God cannot dispatch His first responders, his angels, without you first calling for them in prayer.

Prayer is to always be the first response. You are to continue in prayer and watch with thanksgiving until you receive an answer from your first responder.

Don't grow weary if you don't receive a response right away. Some of your prayers are so powerful and impactful that your angels have to fight a little harder to get the answer to you. Daniel didn't receive an answer for 21 days, but the important thing was he continued in prayer and when the response came it was greater than anything he had ever seen.

Your first responders are coming with answers that will change your life. They are coming with answers that will save your family. They are coming with answers that will heal your land.

Let prayer be your first response in all things, so heaven's first responders may come.

Pray with me:

Dear God, I thank you for this moment. I thank you that you have sent your angels to work on my behalf.

I pray that you would continue to give me the desire to pray. I thank you that you are helping me to grow to a place where prayer is always my first response.

It is so, in Jesus' Name.

What's Next?

Now that you have finished the 30 days, the choice is up to you to continue. I pray that every word inspired you in such a way, that you truly believe in the power of prayer again. I pray that you once again believe that God has chosen you. I pray that you choose God's will for your life with each day that He gives you.
I pray that the spirit of prayer has become you. Above all, I pray that you have found yourself able to walk in the grace of God once more.
As you continue, stay prayerful. Stay watchful. Stay grateful.

Pray with me;
Dear God, I thank you for the completion of this 30 day devotional. I pray now that you would help me to take what I have read and prayed and apply it to my everyday life. I pray that as I have been inspired to live a life of prayer, that someone else will be inspired just the same. Help me God to live in grace that I may please you.
It is so, in Jesus' name.

Made in United States
North Haven, CT
06 June 2023

37362971R00046